Hospital

By Jennifer Colby

21st Century
Junior Library

CHERRY LAKE
Publishing

Published in the United States of America by
Cherry Lake Publishing
Ann Arbor, Michigan
www.cherrylakepublishing.com

Content Adviser: Angela Castro, BSN, RN, CCRN, CEN
Reading Adviser: Marla Conn MS, Ed., Literacy specialist, Read-Ability, Inc.

Photo Credits: © Monkey Business Images/Shutterstock Images, cover, 1, 12, 14, 16;
© Sergey Pazharski/Shutterstock Images, 4; © doraclub/Shutterstock Images, 6;
©gajdamak/Shutterstock Images, 8; ©wang song/Shutterstock Images, 10; © stihii/
Shutterstock Images, 18; © Arina P Habich/Shutterstock Images, 20

Library of Congress Cataloging-in-Publication Data
Names: Colby, Jennifer, 1971- author.
Title: Hospital / by Jennifer Colby.
Description: Ann Arbor : Cherry Lake Publishing, [2016] | Series: 21st
  century junior library. Explore a workplace | Audience: K to grade 3. |
  Includes bibliographical references and index.
Identifiers: LCCN 2015047472 | ISBN 9781634710749 (hardcover) | ISBN 9781634712729 (pbk.) |
ISBN 9781634711739 (pdf) | ISBN 9781634713719 (ebook)
Subjects: LCSH: Hospitals—Juvenile literature. |
  Hospitals—Employees—Juvenile literature. | Medicine—Vocational
  guidance—Juvenile literature.
Classification: LCC RA963.5 .C65 2016 | DDC 610.69—dc23
LC record available at http://lccn.loc.gov/2015047472

Cherry Lake Publishing would like to acknowledge the work of The Partnership for 21st Century Learning.
Please visit *www.p21.org* for more information.

Printed in the United States of America
Corporate Graphics

CONTENTS

5 What Is a Hospital?

9 Hospital Workers

19 Do You Want to Work at a Hospital?

22 Glossary

23 Find Out More

24 Index

24 About the Author

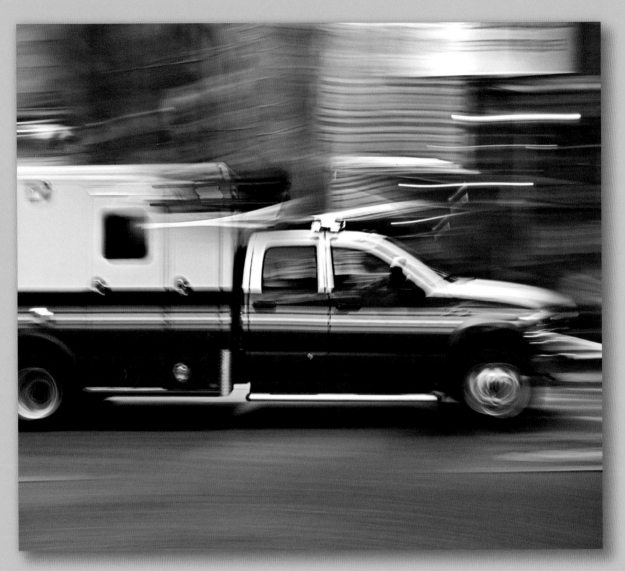

This ambulance is racing to the hospital.

What Is a Hospital?

Do you hear a loud siren? It is an **ambulance**. It takes people to the **hospital**. All cars must move out of the way. The ambulance must get to the hospital fast!

Many babies are born in hospitals.

People go to a hospital when they are sick or hurt. Doctors and nurses help them. Have you been to a hospital? Were you sick? Maybe you visited someone there. Many people work at a hospital. Let's read about some hospital workers.

Think!

Sometimes people are not sick when they are in a hospital. Why is that? Hint: Think about where most babies are born. Pregnant mothers can go to a hospital to have their babies. If this was your answer, you are correct!

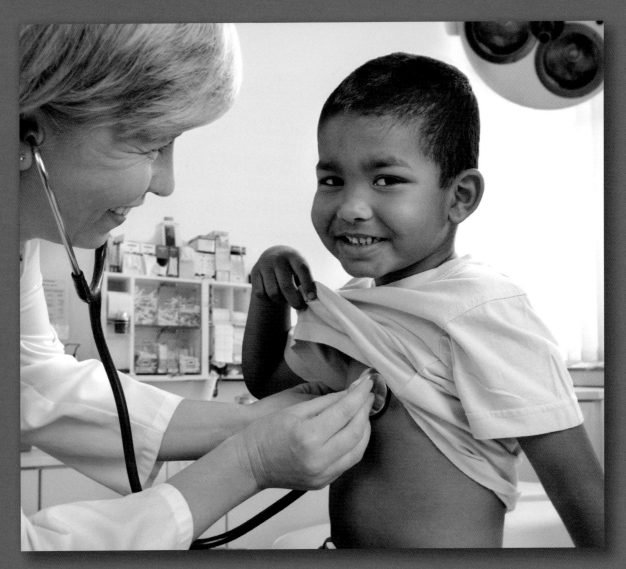

A doctor examines you to find out why you are sick.

Hospital Workers

Many doctors work in hospitals. A doctor finds out why you are sick in order to try and make you better. The doctor will look at you. This is called an examination. The doctor may have some questions about how you feel. The doctor might tell you that you need to stay at the hospital overnight.

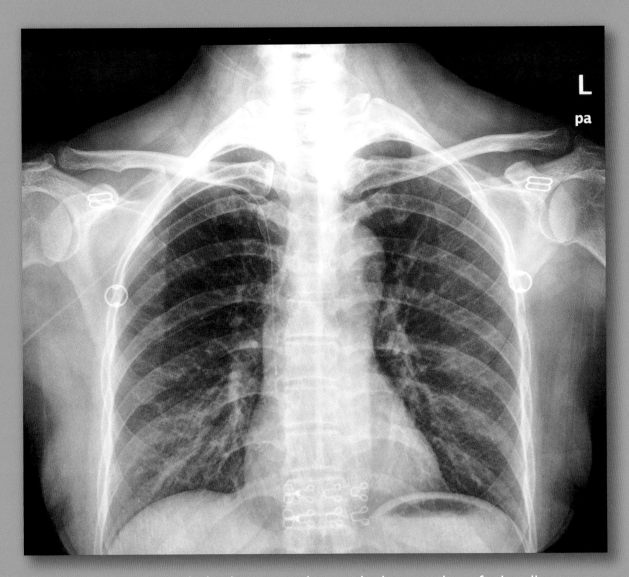

An x-ray can help doctors understand why you don't feel well.

A nurse will help the doctor to take care of you. The nurse may bring you **medicine** if you are having a **fever** or feeling pain. The nurse and other hospital workers will check on you. They want to make sure you are getting better.

You might need to give a sample of your blood or **urine** to see why you don't feel well. Workers will check, or test, the sample. They might also take an **x-ray** of you. An x-ray is a special picture of your body. Doctors will use this information to decide how to make you feel better.

A physical therapist might examine your muscles
to decide which exercises you should do.

Physical therapists help **patients** do special exercises. These exercises help patients move better. There are other kinds of therapists, too. Therapists can help you with speaking and hearing.

Create!

Draw a picture of a hospital worker. Show the worker doing his or her job. Which hospital worker did you choose? Draw the tools the worker needs to do the job.

There are many hospital workers who help to keep patients comfortable.

Being sick or hurt can be scary. **Chaplains** talk with patients. They comfort you by listening. Some hospital workers give you comfort in other ways. You might not even see the jobs they are doing.

Kitchen workers cook meals for patients. They make sure you have healthy food to eat. **Janitors** keep the hospital clean. They wash floors. They scrub rooms. It is important to keep a hospital free of **germs**.

Some hospital workers do their jobs in an office.

Some workers do their jobs in hospital offices. They run the hospital. **Accountants** handle the hospital's money. **Lawyers** make sure the hospital follows rules. A **personnel manager** hires the workers for the hospital. It takes many workers to run a hospital.

Make a Guess!

Guess which jobs most people think of when they think about hospitals. Which three jobs do you think of? Write them on a piece of paper. Ask five people to name three hospital jobs. Write down their answers. Count the total number of each job. Did the most popular jobs match your guesses?

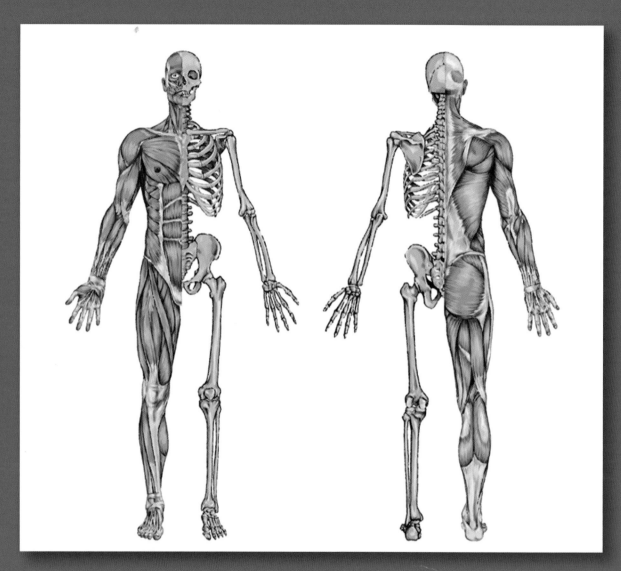

You need to learn about the human body to do many hospital jobs.

Do You Want to Work at a Hospital?

Would you like to work at a hospital? You could be a doctor or a nurse. You can start learning now. Study the human body. How does it work? You can find out what people can do to stay healthy.

Do you like to help make healthy food at home?
You could work in a hospital kitchen.

Hospital workers take care of people. Is that something you enjoy? Find out by helping at home. Help keep your house clean. Help prepare healthy meals.

A hospital can be a great place to work. Learn as much as you can now. You can decide if working at a hospital is right for you!

Ask Questions!

Ask your parents to help you find an adult who works in a hospital. Ask questions about that person's job. What does he or she do? Does the person like that job? Find out what you would have to study in school to do that job.

GLOSSARY

accountants (uh-KOUN-tuhnts) people who are experts at handling money

ambulance (AM-byuh-luhns) a vehicle that takes people who are sick or hurt to the hospital

chaplains (CHAP-luhnz) priests, ministers, rabbis, or people of other faiths who work in hospitals

fever (FEE-vur) a body temperature that is higher than 98.6 degrees Fahrenheit (37 degrees Celsius)

germs (JURMZ) tiny living things that can cause disease

hospital (HAH-spi-tuhl) a place where people who are sick or hurt get help from doctors, nurses, and other workers

janitors (JAN-i-turz) people who clean a building

lawyers (LOI-yurz) people who provide advice about the law

medicine (MED-uh-suhn) a drug used to help sick people get better

patients (PAY-shuhnts) people who are being treated by doctors or other health care workers

personnel manager (pur-suh-NEL MAN-uh-jur) a person who hires and trains workers

physical therapists (FIZ-uh-kuhl THER-uh-pists) people who are trained to help treat muscles and joints that are damaged by sickness or injury

urine (YOOR-uhn) yellow liquid that people pass out of their bodies

x-ray (EKS-rayz) pictures of bones and other organs inside the body

FIND OUT MORE

BOOKS

Heos, Bridget. *Let's Meet a Doctor*. Minneapolis: Millbrook Press, 2013.

Meister, Cari. *Nurses*. Mankato, MN: Jump!, 2014.

WEB SITES

Kids Work!—Inside the Hospital
http://knowitall.org/kidswork/hospital/index.html
Explore a virtual workplace designed to give students an interactive experience.

Nemours—Kids Health: How the Body Works
http://kidshealth.org/kid/htbw/
Learn about the human body.

INDEX

A
accountants, 17
ambulances, 5

B
babies, 7
blood tests, 11

C
chaplains, 15
cleaning, 15, 21

D
doctors, 7, 9, 11, 19

E
examinations, 9
exercises, 13

F
fever, 11

G
germs, 15

H
human body, 19

J
janitors, 15

K
kitchen workers, 15

L
lawyers, 17

M
medicine, 11

N
nurses, 7, 11, 19

O
offices, 17

P
patients, 13, 15
physical therapists, 13

T
tests, 11
therapists, 13

X
x-rays, 11

ABOUT THE AUTHOR

Jennifer Colby is the author of many books for children. She is a high school librarian in Michigan. She once went to a hospital when she broke her arm.